THE Sleepover Joke BOOK

Sandy Ransford

illustrated by
Emily Bannister

PUFFIN BOOKS

PUFFIN BOOKS

Published by the Penguin Group
Penguin Books Ltd, 80 Strand, London WC2R 0RL, England
Penguin Putnam Inc., 375 Hudson Street, New York, New York 10014, USA
Penguin Books Australia Ltd, 250 Camberwell Road, Camberwell,
Victoria 3124, Australia
Penguin Books Canada Ltd, 10 Alcorn Avenue, Toronto, Ontario, Canada M4V 3B2
Penguin Books India (P) Ltd, 11 Community Centre, Panchsheel Park,
New Delhi – 110 017, India
Penguin Books (NZ) Ltd, Cnr Rosedale and Airborne Roads, Albany, Auckland,
New Zealand
Penguin Books (South Africa) (Pty) Ltd, 24 Sturdee Avenue, Rosebank 2196,
South Africa

Penguin Books Ltd, Registered Offices: 80 Strand, London WC2R 0RL, England

www.penguin.com

First published 2003
3

Text copyright © Sandy Ransford, 2003
Illustrations copyright © Emily Bannister, 2003
All rights reserved

The moral right of the author and illustrator has been asserted

Set in Smile ICG Medium and Myriad Cn Bold

Made and printed in England by Clays Ltd, St Ives plc

British Library Cataloguing in Publication Data
A CIP catalogue record for this book is available from the British Library

ISBN 0–141–31606–3

THE
Sleepover
Joke
BOOK

Sandy Ransford was born in Sheffield, and trained and worked as a physiotherapist before entering publishing. She has worked as a sub-editor, an editor, a reporter and, of course, a writer.

She has written over seventy books, including thirty joke books, puzzle books, titles on horses and riding, conservation, games and activities, fashion, spies, magic, dogs and cats.

She is married to an architect, and the houshold also includes a horse, two ponies, two pygmy goats, two sheep and two cats.

CONTENTS

'YOU ARE INVITED . . .'

IT'S SLEEPOVER TIME! SO GRAB YOUR PYJAMAS AND SLEEPING BAG AND COME ON ROUND . . .

Knock, knock.
Who's there?
Sarah.
Sarah who?
Sarah sleepover in this house tonight?

Why do mushrooms make great sleepover guests?
Because they're such fungis.

Knock, knock.
Who's there?
Ivan.
Ivan who?
Ivan new pair of pyjamas, do you like them?

What happens if you eat too much chocolate at a sleepover?
You turn into a cocoa-nut.

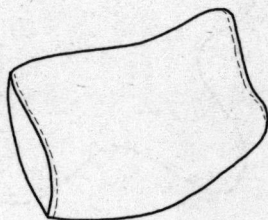

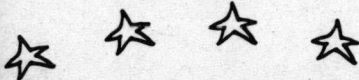

JILLY: Is it all right if I stay the night?
MILLY'S MUM: Yes, but you'll have to make your own bed.
JILLY: That's OK, I have to do that at home.
MILLY'S MUM: Well, here's a hammer and some nails. You'll find the wood in the garage.

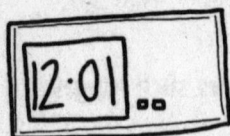

Why is an elephant such a good sleepover guest?
He makes a great impression.

Why don't gnomes like sleepovers?
They suffer from gnome-sickness.

Which dinosaur should you never invite to your sleepover?
A brontosnorus.

How can you tell if there's an elephant in your bed?
Your head touches the ceiling.

What do you get if you cross a ghost with a packet of crisps?
Snacks that go 'crunch' in the night.

GUEST: Do you have running water in your bedroom?
SUSIE: Only when it rains.

What goes right up to your friend's house but never goes in?
The front path.

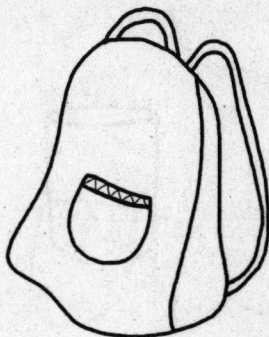

SALLY: Last time I went to Sarah's she had so many friends there I had to sleep on a door resting on two chairs.
SHEILA: Wasn't that very uncomfortable?
SALLY: No, but it was rather draughty round the letterbox.

DON: Shall I tell you the joke about the bed?
RON: Yes.
DON: I can't, it hasn't been made yet.

What's the difference between an American sleepover and a British sleepover?
About 3,000 miles!

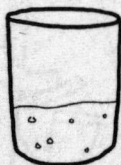

JOE: What's the difference between a sleepover and a matterbaby?
MO: What's a matterbaby?
JOE: Nothing, but thanks for asking.

Knock, knock.
Who's there?
Carmen.
Carmen who?
Carmen and hurry up, it's time
to go to Jenny's sleepover!

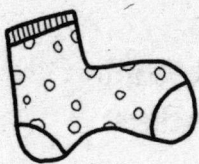

Knock, knock.
Who's there?
Java.
Java who?
Java dressing gown I could
borrow?

Knock, knock.
Who's there?
Havana.
Havana who?
Havana great time at my
sleepover!

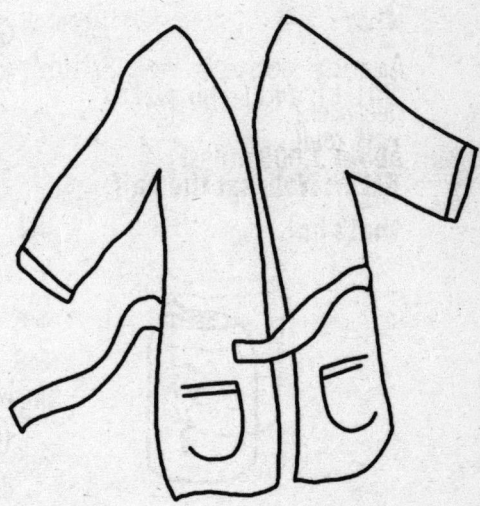

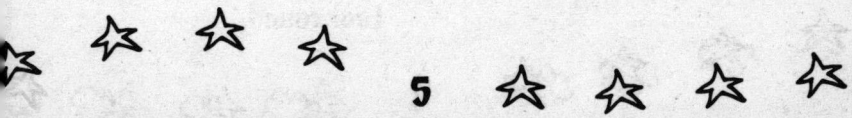

FEAST OF FUN

HOPE YOU'RE FEELING HUNGRY, IT'S TIME TO GET STARTED ON THE FOOD . . .

Knock, knock.
Who's there?
Wicked.
Wicked who?
Wicked order some pizzas
now.

Knock, knock.
Who's there?
Gorilla.
Gorilla who?
Gorilla the pizzas to melta
the cheese.

SHELLEY: Yuck! This pizza's
half cold!
**KELLY: Well, eat the half
that's hot.**

What can a whole pizza do
that half a pizza cannot
do?
Look round.

Who invented spaghetti?
Someone who used his noodle.

What's the best way to eat spaghetti?
Put it in your mouth.

What did the spaghetti say to the tomatoes?
'That's enough of your sauce.'

What's the best day to eat fish and chips?
Fry-day.

Knock, knock.
Who's there?
Harriet.
Harriet who?
Harriet all my pasta and now I'm starving.

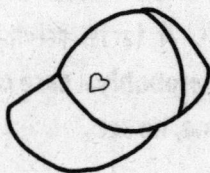

Where were chips first fried?
In Greece.

Knock, knock.
Who's there?
Arthur.
Arthur who?
Arthur any more chips in the pan?

JO: What's the matter with this fish? It tastes peculiar.
MO: It's probably a case of long time, no sea.

BILL: Fish is supposed to be good for your brains.
WILL: I know. I eat lots of it.
BILL: So much for that theory, then.

Why are cooks cruel?
Because they batter fish and beat eggs.

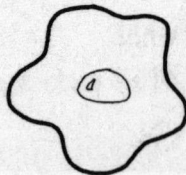

JOHN: Would you like seconds?
DON: No thanks, I'm too young to die.

BERYL: Are you a good cook?
CHERYL: No. Last night I
burnt the salad.

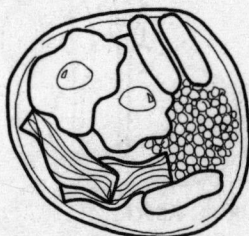

Why was there a button in
the salad?
It came off the jacket
potato.

GILL: Are slugs good to eat?
BILL: Why do you ask?
GILL: There was one in your
salad but it's gone now.

What's worse than finding a
slug in your salad?
Finding half a slug!

What's green and white and bounces?
A spring onion.

WESLEY: Why aren't you
eating your hamburger?
**LESLEY: I'm waiting for the
mustard to cool.**

What did the potato say
when it was wrapped up and
put in the oven?
'Foiled again!'

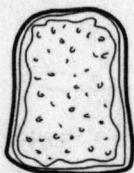

'Will our hamburgers be long?'
'No, round.'

What do you get if you cross
a bee with minced beef?
A humburger.

Why did Harry hit his plate with a sausage?
Because he wanted bangers and smash.

MUM: Eat up your meat,
it's full of iron.
**MILLY: No wonder it's so
tough.**

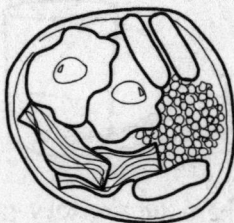

Why is roast pork like an old
radio?
**They both have a lot of
crackling.**

How do you make a chicken
stew?
**Keep it waiting around for a
year or two.**

Why did the family eat all
the white meat off the
chicken?
To make a clean breast of it.

How do you know if you've eaten a
battery hen?
The taste is shocking.

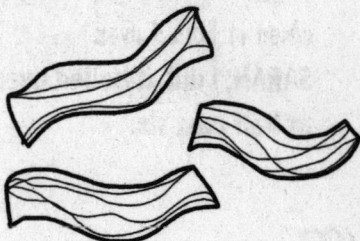

MUM: Eat up your cabbage, it will put colour in your cheeks.
MANDY: But I don't want green cheeks!

What kind of food should
athletes eat?
Runner beans.

Where did the baby cabbage
come from?
The stalk brought it.

ZOE: Oh dear, it's UFO time
again.
**CHLOE: What do you mean,
UFO time?**
ZOE: Unidentified Frying
Objects for supper.

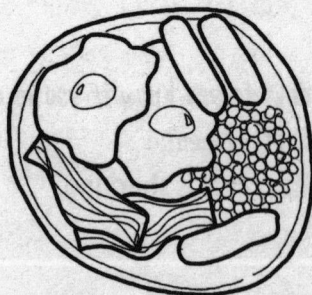

MUM: I thought I told you to
watch the rice and tell me
when it boiled over.
**SARAH: I did, it boiled over
at half past six.**

MUM: Wash your hands, Danny, I want you to cut the sandwiches.
DANNY: Don't worry, I'll make them from brown bread.

MUM: Why is your little sister crying?
PETE: Because I won't give her my sandwich.
MUM: But what about her own sandwich?
PETE: She cried when I ate that too.

FREDDIE: What sort of sandwiches do you like best?
TEDDY: Tongue.
FREDDIE: Ugh! I couldn't eat something that had come out of an animal's mouth!
TEDDY: Well, what kind do you like best?
FREDDIE: Egg.

What musical instrument goes
with cheese?
Pickle-o.

How do Welsh people eat
cheese?
Caerphilly.

JANE: Have you got some of that two-handed cheese?
WAYNE: What do you mean, 'two-handed cheese'?
JANE: The sort you eat with one hand while you hold your
nose with the other.

MUM: Don't eat so quickly,
Roger.
**ROGER: But, Mum, I might
lose my appetite unless I do.**

RUPERT: I don't like cheese
with holes in.
**MUM: Then leave the holes
at the side of your plate and
eat the rest.**

Why are grapes never lonely?
**Because they hang around
in bunches.**

What's round and can't sit
down?
A seatless satsuma.

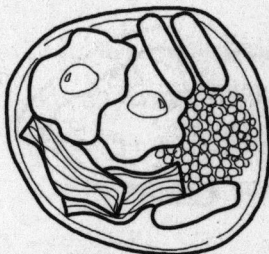

How do you make a banana split?
Cut it in half.

How do you make a jam
turnover?
Push it off the table.

How do you make an apple
puff?
Chase it round the garden.

What do you get if you cross apples with a plane?
Pie in the sky.

CHARLIE: Do you like baked apples?
DAD: Yes. Why do you ask?
CHARLIE: The orchard's on fire.

What are the best things to put in a pie?
Your teeth!

What's yellow, thick and dangerous?
Shark-infested custard.

Why did the blancmange wobble?
Because it saw the milk shake.

What flour do pixies use to make cakes?
Elf-raising flour.

What cake wanted to rule the world?
Attila the Bun.

What do you get if you cross gunpowder with eggs?
A boom-meringue.

What should you do with rock cakes?
Take your pick.

MUM: How many times do I have to tell you to leave the chocolate eclairs alone?
JEFF: No more, I've eaten them all.

MANY HAPPY RETURNS!

SLEEPOVERS MAKE GREAT BIRTHDAY TREATS . . .

12·01

BILL: When's your birthday?
BEN: 26th April.
BILL: Which year?
BEN: Every year.

Knock, knock.
Who's there?
Farmer.
Farmer who?
Farmer birthday I got all my friends round for a sleepover!

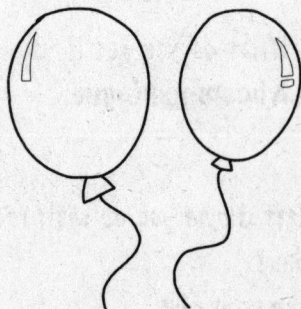

GLENDA: What did you get for your birthday?
BRENDA: A year older!

JACK: Would you like to come to my birthday party next week?
JILL: **Oh, yes, please. What's your address?**
JACK: Number 25 Laburnum Avenue. Just press the bell with your elbow.
JILL: **Why with my elbow?**
JACK: Well, you won't be coming empty-handed, will you?

Little Johnny was on his way to Sergio's birthday sleepover when his mum realized he was trying to cross a busy road in a dangerous place. She rushed up to him and said, 'What are you doing trying to cross here? Don't you know there's a zebra crossing just round the corner?'

'I hope it's having better luck than me,' replied Johnny.

PADDY: Why didn't you go to Jane's party?
MADDY: **Well, the invitation said from six to nine, and I'm ten.**

What did the spider give her
husband for his birthday?
Four pairs of trainers.

Where's the best place to
have a party on a ship?
Where the funnel be.

DOLLY: Why didn't you write
anything on my birthday
card?
MOLLY: **Because then you'd
realize I can't spell.**

DAVE: I dreamt I took the most beautiful girl in the world to Rick's party.
MAVE: Really? What did I wear?

William got a new bike for his birthday and raced round the garden on it, showing off to his friends. He rode round with his feet off the pedals. 'Look, no feet,' he called out.

Then he rode round and took his hands off the handlebars. 'Look, no hands,' he shouted. He disappeared for a short while, but then came round again. 'Mmm, look, no teef,' he mumbled.

Billy's birthday sleepover was in January. When it came to going home time, Susie complained that she couldn't find her boots. 'Aren't these yours?' asked Billy's mum.

'No, they're not,' replied Susie. 'Mine were covered in snow.'

Annie's birthday sleepover was also in the middle of winter and snow lay on the ground. Before tea, the children all went sledging in the park. 'Now, Annie,' said her mum, 'remember you must share your sledge with your friends.'

'OK,' said Annie. She turned to her friend Ali. 'You can share my sledge. I'll have it going downhill, and you can have it going uphill.'

Knock, Knock.
Who's there?
Genoa.
Genoa who?
Genoa the steps to this new dance?

What do Eskimos sing at a birthday sleepover?
'Freeze a jolly good fellow.'

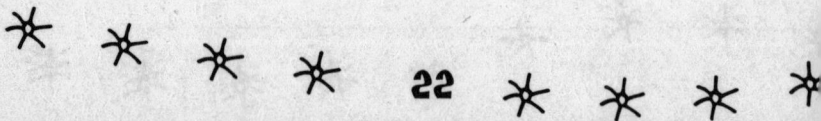

What do you get if you cross a birthday cake with a tin of baked beans?
A cake that blows out its own candles.

Knock, knock.
Who's there?
Police.
Police who?
Police let me in, I was invited.

Knock, knock.
Who's there?
Passion.
Passion who?
Just passion by and heard a party going on.

Knock, knock.
Who's there?
Heaven.
Heaven who?
Heaven seen you for such a long time.

Young Gail was given a recorder and a bottle of perfume for her birthday. The following day her parents invited the neighbours in for tea, and Gail sat between them.

She chatted happily about her birthday and all the presents she had received, and told them cheerfully, 'If you hear a little noise, and smell a little smell, it's me.'

HIL: Did you miss me when I was away?
PHIL: When were you away?

How can you make dumb Donald laugh at your birthday sleepover?
Tell him a joke the week before.

BOBBY: I've brought you a box of your favourite chocolates for your birthday.
NOBBY: But the box is half empty!
BOBBY: Yes, well, they're my favourites too.

DARREN: What would you like for your birthday?
SHARON: I'd like a surprise.
DARREN: OK – booo!

Len, Ben and Ken got into a fight at Ken's birthday party.
'You're so stupid, Ben,' said Len.
'That's not very nice,' said Ken.
'You should say you're sorry.'
'OK,' said Len. 'I'm sorry you're so stupid, Ben.'

How does someone know when they're getting old?
Their birthday cake costs less than the candles.

How do baby hens dance at a birthday party?
Chick to chick.

How do hedgehogs dance at a birthday party?
Very carefully!

What dance do ducks do?
The quackstep.

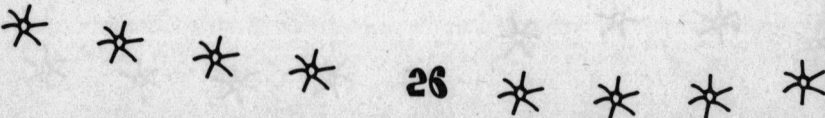

What do you call the *Star Wars* character who's a very good dancer?
Darth Raver.

What dance should you do at a party at the end of the summer?
The tan-go.

Why is a horse such a bad dancer?
Because he's got two left feet.

Knock, knock.
Who's there?
Bertha.
Bertha who?
Happy Bertha-day!

MEET THE FAMILY

DO YOU WISH YOUR EMBARRASSING FAMILY WOULD DISAPPEAR WHEN YOUR FRIENDS ARE ROUND? WELL, SOME FAMILIES ARE EVEN WORSE ...

ZOE: Does your mum have a dishwasher?
CHLOE: Yes, my dad!

VAL: My mum loves our house. She says it hasn't a flaw.
SAL: Whatever do you walk on, then?

FREDDIE: May I have another apple, please?
MUM: No, you can't. They don't grow on trees, you know.

MUM: I stopped a strange man in the street yesterday.
DAUGHTER: What happened?
MUM: I thought he was your dad. As I explained when he turned round, his head looked just like Dad's behind.

MUM: If you eat up your greens you'll grow up to be beautiful.
LAUREN: Why didn't you eat your greens when you were young?

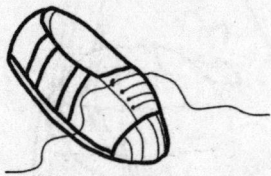

Despite his mother's warnings, Bobby insisted on climbing the tree in the garden.
'All right,' she said, 'but if you fall and break your leg don't come running to me.'

Why did Grandad wear all his clothes to paint the garden shed?
Because the instructions said, 'Put on three coats.'

DAD: Nigel! Come here! I'll teach you to kick footballs at my greenhouse!
NIGEL: I wish you would, I keep missing.

'Why is your sister so small?'
'She's my half-sister.'

BIG SISTER: What's the weather like?
LITTLE SISTER: I can't tell, it's too foggy to see.

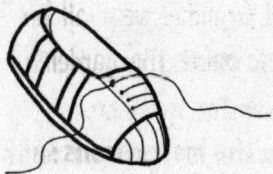

MUM: Have you put your shoes on yet?
KAREN: Yes, Mum, all except one.

TINA: What kind of car does your dad drive?
GINA: I'm not sure, but it starts with T.
TINA: Really? Ours starts with petrol!

RICKY: How long did it take your brother to learn to drive?
NICKY: Oh, about three and a half cars.

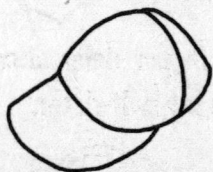

DAD: Will you just hop out of the car and tell me if my indicators are working, Pat?
PAT: OK. Yes, no, yes, no, yes, no.

Dad was stopped by a traffic policeman for speeding. 'Why were you going so fast?' the policeman asked. **'I was trying to get home before the car ran out of petrol,'** Dad explained.

MUM: Didn't you see the 30 mph limit sign?
DAD: No, I was going too fast to notice it.

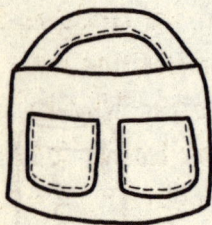

On another occasion, Mum was stopped and the policeman told her she'd been driving at 95 mph. **'That's impossible,'** she protested. **'I've only been in the car twenty minutes.'**

Dad's driving terrified Mum, who complained whenever he took a corner too fast. **'Don't worry,'** said Dad. **'Do what I do.'**
'What's that?' asked Mum. **'Close your eyes.'**

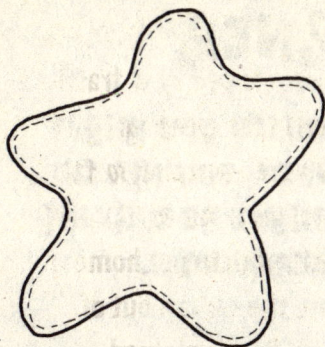

Annie's little sister was having problems putting on her shoes. 'It's because you're trying to put them on the wrong feet,' said Annie. **'But these are the only feet I've got,'** replied her sister **sadly.**

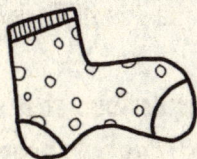

Cousin Charlie, who was not very bright, was struggling to move a wardrobe from one room to another. 'Why don't you get your brother to help you?' asked Clara.
'He is helping,' replied Charlie. **'He's inside carrying the clothes.'**

33

PETS' CORNER

IT'S NOT JUST CRAZY FAMILIES YOU MIGHT ENCOUNTER AT A SLEEPOVER. YOU NEVER KNOW WHAT CREATURES MIGHT BE LURKING IN YOUR FRIEND'S BEDROOM ...

When might you have a narrow squeak at a sleepover?
When you tread on your friend's pet mouse.

What did the mouse say when it broke its front teeth?
'Hard cheese.'

What do you get if you cross your friend's mouse with an elephant?
Huge holes in the skirting-board.

What do you get if you cross your friend's hamster with a bowl of strawberries?
Hamster jam.

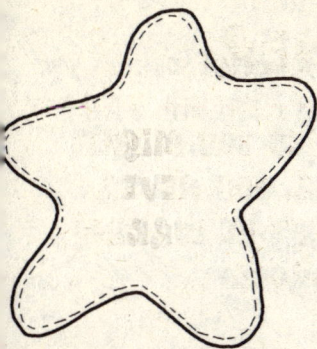

What did Jenny do when someone stole her canary?
Phoned the Flying Squad.

What did Andy get when someone ran the lawnmower over his pet canary?
Shredded tweet.

What did Abby's parrot eat?
Polyfilla.

What would you get if you crossed Abby's parrot with an elephant?
A bird with a very dirty cage.

What do you get if you spill your tea on your friend's pet rabbit?
A hot, cross bunny.

What do you get if you cross your friend's pet rabbit with a leek?
A bunion.

What did Biddy's dog say when it sat on a sheet of sandpaper?
'Ruff.'

DILLY: Does your dog like children?
TILLY: Yes, but he prefers meat and gravy.

MO: Our dog is just like one of the family.
JO: Really? Who does he look like?

FREDDIE: Every day my dog and I go for a tramp in the woods.
FREDA: Does the dog enjoy it?
FREDDIE: Yes, but the tramp's getting a bit fed up.

What would you get if you crossed
Gina's sheepdog with a plant?
A collie-flower.

JENNY: Why is your dog
called Isaiah?
**PENNY: Because one of his
eyes is 'igher than the other.**

Did you hear about the dog
that lived on onions?
**His bark was worse than
his bite.**

What goes tick, tock, woof?
A watch-dog.

Why did Penny's dog howl?
**Because it barked up the
wrong tree.**

JANE: My dog has no nose.
WAYNE: How does he smell?
JANE: Terrible!

What do you get if you cross
Liam's dog with a hairdresser?
A shampoodle.

What do you get if you cross
Laura's dog with a telephone?
A golden receiver.

JILLY: Why is your cat called
Ben Hur?
**BILLY: He was just called Ben
until she had kittens.**

What happened when Jane's
cat ate a ball of wool?
She had mittens.

Why did Sally's cat join the Red Cross?
It wanted to be a first-aid kit.

What do you call a cat from the Wild West?
A posse.

What did Ned's cat do when it swallowed the cheese?
Waited at a mousehole with baited breath.

What do you get if you cross an alley cat with a canary?
A peeping tom.

What happened when Fred's snake caught a cold?
She adder viper nose.

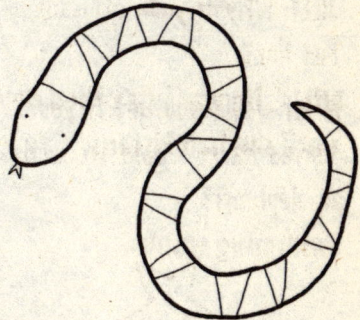

What's green and slimy and goes hith?
A snake with a lisp.

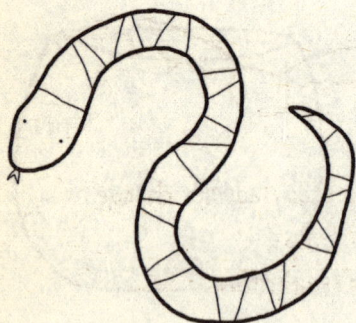

FIRST SNAKE: Are we supposed to be poisonous?
SECOND SNAKE: I don't think so. Why do you ask?
FIRST SNAKE: I just bit my lip.

Why can't you play a joke on a snake?
You can't pull its leg.

What is the world's most valuable fish?
A goldfish.

What would you get if you crossed Harry's goldfish with an elephant?
Swimming trunks.

Where did Billy's frog keep its money?
In a river bank.

What happened when Billy's frog parked his car on a double yellow line?
It got toad away.

Where do tadpoles change into frogs?
In a croakroom.

What do you call two spiders who are recently married?
Newly webs.

What would you get if you crossed Keith's tarantula with a computer?
A very large web site.

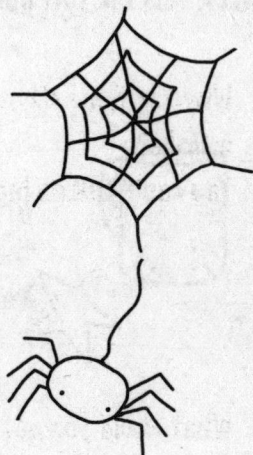

What's long-legged and sticky?
Johnny's stick insect.

LOG ON

HOW ABOUT SOME FUN WITH THAT COMPUTER?

BILLY: How are you getting on with exploring the Internet?
GILLY: Surf far, surf good.

What do keen surfers of the Internet drink?
Netscafé.

RONALD: Do you have an address for the strawberry jam web site?
DONALD: Yes, but don't spread it around.

JUDY: Have you seen
www.skeletons.com?
**RUDY: Yes, it's a rattling
good web site.**

What did Long John Silver's
parrot say when it used the
Internet?
'Pcs of eight, pcs of eight.'

What sits in the middle of
the World Wide Web?
A very, very large spider.

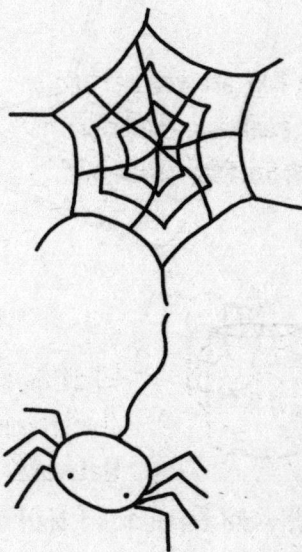

How do dustmen surf the
Web?
They use the binternet.

How do you mend a broken
web site?
You use stick-e-tape.

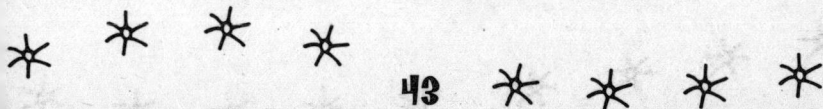

43

Why didn't the boy mouse
get on with the girl mouse?
They just didn't click.

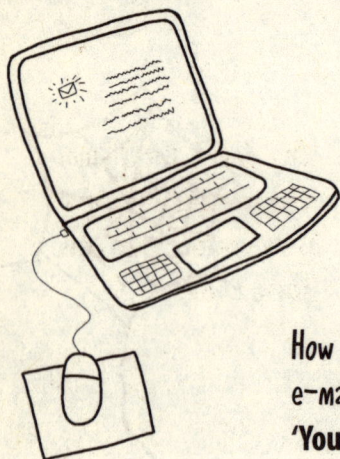

How do sheep sign their
e-mails?
'Ewes sincerely.'

How do robots sign their
e-mails?
'Yours tincerely.'

Why did Bernie paint black and white squares
on his computer screen?
So he could check his e-mail.

When do e-mails stop being in black and
white?
When they're read.

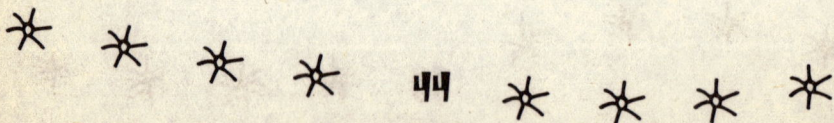

How do prawns type e-mails?
With fish fingers.

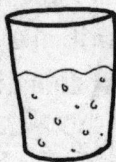

Why didn't the Vikings
send e-mails?
**They preferred to use
Norse Code.**

What do you get if you cross a
computer with a hamburger?
A big Mac.

Why did the gardener put a
raincoat over his fruit tree?
**Someone told him to get an
Apple Mac.**

DAD: Do you want some help using that computer?
DAUGHTER: No thanks, I can muck it up all on my own.

GRAHAM: Would you buy a second-hand computer?
GEORGE: No, I can only type with one hand as it is.

Did you hear about the two computers who wanted to raise a family?
They longed to hear the patter of tinny feet.

Why did the computer fail its driving test?
It crashed so often.

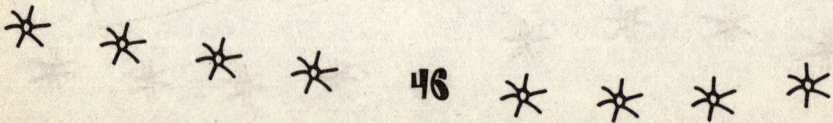

What do you get if you take
your computer to an ice rink?
A slipped disk.

What do you get if you cross
a computer with Michael
Schumacher?
**A computer that crashes at
200 mph.**

What notice did the computer
novice have stuck on his
machine?
**'Abandon hope all ye who
press ENTER here.'**

What did dumb Donald say
when told the computer would
cut his work in half?
'Great, I'll have two of them.'

ON-SCREEN

IT'S TIME TO GRAB THE REMOTE AND SNUGGLE UP ON THE SOFA. WHAT'S ON?

ELLA: Do you know anyone who's been on the telly?
BELLA: My little brother did once but he can use a potty now.

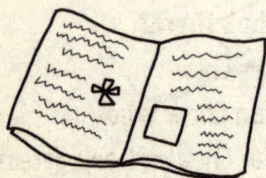

LYNNE: What's on the telly tonight?
GWYN: The usual.
LYNNE: What's that?
GWYN: A bowl of fruit and a vase of flowers.

BOB: I agree with Dad, TV will never replace newspapers.
ROB: Why do you say that?
BOB: Have you ever tried wrapping fish and chips in a TV?

JOHN: I agree with people who say television causes violence.
DON: Why?
JOHN: Because every time I try to change channels my brother hits me.

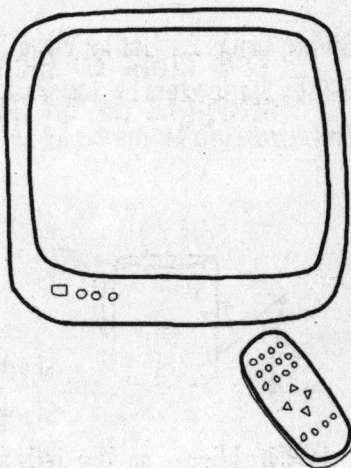

Knock, knock.
Who's there?
Weed.
Weed who?
Weed like to watch the telly, please.

Knock knock.
Who's there?
Watson.
Watson who?
Watson the box tonight?

Knock, knock.
Who's there?
Evan Chew.
Evan Chew who?
Evan Chew got any decent videos to watch?

Have a look at these strange video titles:

Giving Great Parties by Maud D. Merrier
Happy Sleepovers by Tamara Sanotherday
Embarrassing Moments by Lucy Lastic

Skydiving by Hugo First
Sleepless Nights by Constance Nora
Winning the Lottery by Ivor Fortune

Quick Breakfasts by Roland Butter
Firework Displays by Dinah Mite
Delicious Cheeses by Della Katesssen

Walking Home by Miss D. Buss
Putting Up Shelves by Andy Mann
Keeping the House Tidy by Anita Room

Meet Me in the Park by Wendy Classisover
A Bump on the Head by I. C. Stars
Looking Forward to the Weekend by Gladys Friday

Walking to Australia by Willy Makit and Betty Wont
How Hannibal Crossed the Alps by Rhoda Nelephant
Vegetable Gardening by Rosa Beans

Nursery Rhymes by Polly Putthekettleon
Laying Carpets by Walter Wall
Picking Strawberries by Phil D. Basket

Where Shall We Go? by Ivor Nidea
Crossing the River by Romeo Verr
Catching the Early Train by Justin Thyme
Creating Monsters by Frank N. Stein

SHIVERS DOWN THE SPINE

WHAT BETTER THAN SOME CREEPY STORIES TO TELL IN THE MIDDLE OF THE DARK, DARK NIGHT?

What did the ghoul say when it entered the mortuary?
'Is any body there?'

Where do ghosts get their jokes from?
Crypt writers.

How does a ghost begin a letter?
'Tomb it may concern.'

Why was there a fence round the cemetery?
People were dying to get in.

Eddie and Neddy went out to collect conkers one autumn afternoon. They headed for the local graveyard, where there were lots of horse-chestnut trees. They managed to pick up a good bagful, and sat down on a gravestone to share them out. As they were doing so, Eddie dropped a couple, which rolled down towards the gate at the graveyard's entrance.

It was beginning to get dark when Polly decided to take a short cut through the graveyard on her way home. She felt a bit uneasy about doing so, and stopped in her tracks when she heard voices saying, 'That's one for you, this is one for me.'

She rushed out into the street and bumped into a policeman. 'Help!' she screamed. 'There are ghosts in the churchyard and they're sharing out the bodies!'

The policeman accompanied her to the gate, where they stopped and listened.

Clearly through the evening air they heard a voice saying, 'That's one for you, this is one for me, and don't forget those two down by the gate.'

Why did the ghost look in the mirror?
To see if he still wasn't there.

Where do ghosts swim?
In the Dead Sea.

Where do ghosts go at Christmas?
To the phantomime.

Who might you meet on a ghost train?
The ticket inspectre.

What does a ghost call his mum and dad?
Transparents.

Did you hear about the stupid ghost? It climbed over walls and opened doors.

Knock, knock.
Who's there?
Luke.
Luke who?
Luke behind you, there's a ghost!

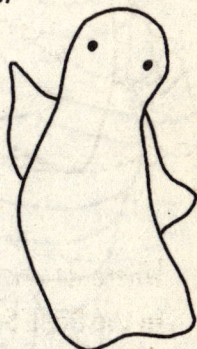

What do you call a ghost who haunts a hospital?
A surgical spirit.

Why was the little Egyptian boy confused?
Because his daddy was a mummy.

What do mummies wear on their finger ends?
Nile varnish.

Why are mummies good at keeping secrets?
They keep everything under wraps.

Which ancient Egyptian ruler was very good at washing up?
Pharoah Liquid.

What did the boy mummy say to the girl mummy?
'Embalmy about you.'

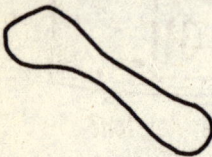

Who sailed the phantom ship?
A skeleton crew.

How did the skeleton know it was going to rain?
He could feel it in his bones.

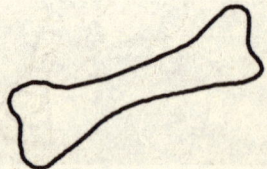

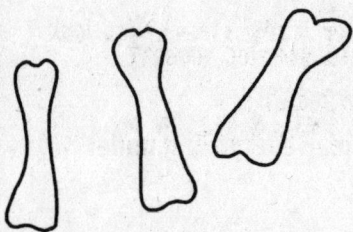

Why didn't the skeleton go to the ball?
Because he had no body to dance with.

What do you call a friendly skeleton?
A bony crony.

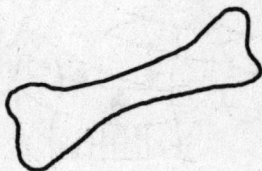

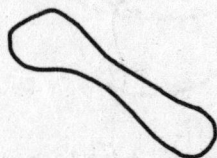

What do you call a skeleton who's a very good detective?
Sherlock Bones.

What do skeletons buy at fêtes?
Rattle tickets.

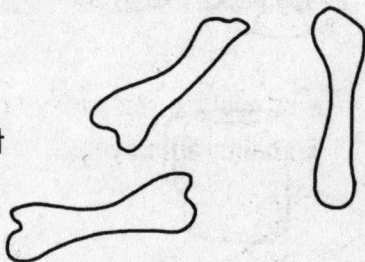

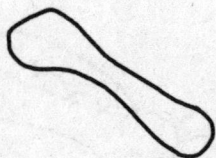

What is a skeleton?
Someone who wears his insides outside.

Two zombies bumped into each other in the street. 'You look tired,' said the first.

'I am,' answered the second. 'In fact, I'm dead on my feet.'

Who does a zombie take out on a date?
Any old pal he can dig up.

What do vampires eat for breakfast?
Ready neck.

What do vampires have each morning between breakfast and lunch?
A coffin break.

What's a vampire's favourite soup?
Scream of tomato.

What did the young vampire
say to his mum at bedtime?
'Read me a gory.'

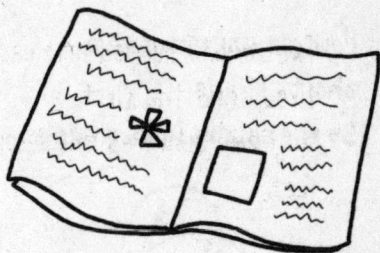

Why did the vampire eat lots of mints?
Because he had bat breath.

How do you join Count
Dracula's fan club?
**Send in your name, address
and blood group.**

How does a werewolf sign his
letters?
'Best vicious.'

How can you recognize a
ghost's bicycle?
By the spooks in its wheels.

How do ghosts keep their
feet dry?
They wear ghouloshes.

If you're a ghost, what's the difference
between a shroud and a person?
One you wear, the other you were.

NEW PUPIL: Is this school
haunted?
**OLD PUPIL: I don't think so.
Why do you ask?**
NEW PUPIL: The head teacher
is always going on about the
school spirit.

What's the difference between a musician and a corpse?
One composes, the other decomposes.

What do Hungarian ghosts eat?
Ghoulash.

What do you call two corpses in a belfry?
Dead ringers.

What's a ghost's favourite dance?
The last vaults.

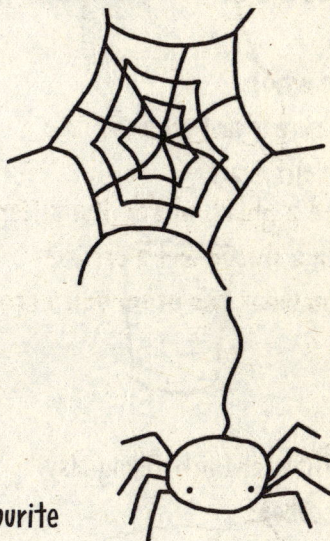

What do Italian ghosts eat?
Spookhetti.

MIDNIGHT FEASTS

PHEW! AFTER ALL THAT EXCITEMENT IT'S TIME FOR A BIT MORE TO EAT . . .

Knock, knock.
Who's there?
Sam.
Sam who?
Sam sweets and crisps for our midnight feast.

What happens if you wrap your sandwiches in your favourite comic?
You get crumby jokes.

What sandwich filling plays snooker?
A cue-cumber.

What's white or brown outside and green inside?
A frog sandwich.

What's yellow and brown and hairy?
Cheese on toast dropped on the carpet.

Knock, knock.
Who's there?
Omar.
Omar who?
Omar goodness, what a feast!

GORDON: Why did you mop up your tea with your cake?
GLORIA: Well, it is sponge cake.

What nut has no shell?
A doughnut.

JACK: I think there's a burglar in the kitchen eating the cake my sister made for our midnight feast.
ZAK: Shall I call the police or an ambulance?

What do you get if you cross sugar and egg white with a monkey?
A meringue utan.

Knock, knock.
Who's there?
Doughnut.
Doughnut who?
Doughnut come near me, I can't stand you!

What do you get if you cross a strawberry with an elk?
Strawberry mousse.

What do you get if you cross a tub of ice cream with a football team?
Aston Vanilla.

ANNE: Why do you like alphabet soup?
DAN: I like to read while I'm eating.

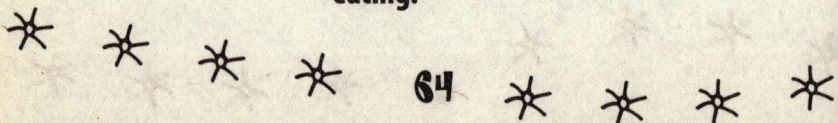

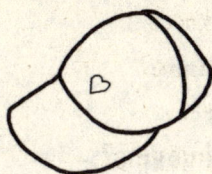

What do computer programmers
eat at midnight feasts?
Microchips.

What's a monster's favourite
drink?
Demonade.

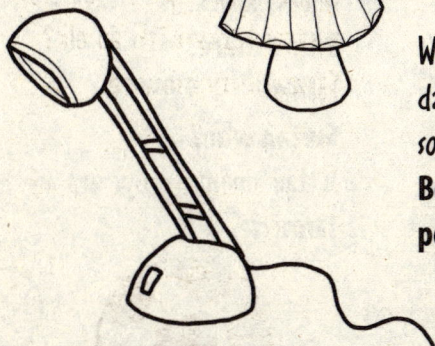

Why did the boy stick his
dad's fingers in the light
socket?
**Because he wanted fizzy
pop.**

What's a frog's favourite
drink?
Croaka-cola.

What would you call five
bottles of lemonade?
A pop group.

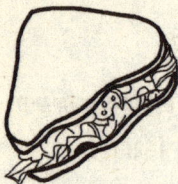

Knock, knock.
Who's there?
Pizza.
Pizza who?
Pizza cake's all I want.

Knock, knock.
Who's there?
Orange.
Orange who?
Orange you glad I brought
that chocolate cake?

Knock, knock.
Who's there?
Sultan.
Sultan who?
Sultan vinegar crisps are my
favourite.

Knock, knock.
Who's there?
Curry.
Curry who?
Curry this plate of biscuits
for me, will you?

Why did the biscuit cry?
**Because his mother had
been a wafer so long.**

What did the biscuits say to the almonds?
'You're nuts and we're crackers.'

What's the best thing to put in an ice-cream sundae?
A spoon!

What's the difference between a chocolate biscuit and an elephant?
You can't dip an elephant in your tea.

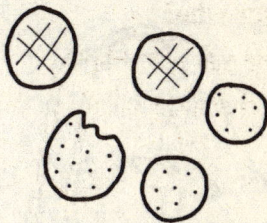

How do you start a jelly race?
You say, 'Get set.'

What did the boy who had jelly in one ear and custard in the other say?
'Can you speak louder, please, I'm a trifle deaf.'

What do jelly babies wear on their feet?
Gum boots.

What's made of chocolate and found in the sea?
An oyster egg.

What do you get if you cross the pupils in the top class with an underground train?
A tube of Smarties.

How do you make a lemon drop?
Shake the tree hard.

Knock, knock.
Who's there?
Arthur.
Arthur who?
Arthur any more chocolates left?

HORACE: What's the difference between a chocolate bar and dog dirt?
MAURICE: **I don't know. What is the difference between a chocolate bar and dog dirt?**
HORACE: If you don't know I shan't send you out to buy any chocolate!

Knock, knock.
Who's there?
Felix.
Felix who?
Felix my lollipop again I'll thump him.

Knock, knock.
Who's there?
Philip.
Philip who?
Philip my plate, I'm starving!

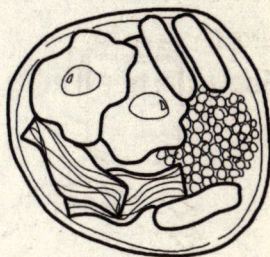

JOKES TO KEEP YOU AWAKE

TRYING TO STAY AWAKE ALL NIGHT? TELL THESE JOKES TO YOUR FRIENDS AND THEY'LL BE GIGGLING SO MUCH THEY'LL NEVER GET TO SLEEP!

Knock, knock.
Who's there?
Tailor.
Tailor who?
Tailor me a good joke!

Knock, knock.
Who's there?
Will Young.
Will Young who?
Will Young Billy please come in for his tea?

HANSEL: What's your phone number?
GRETEL: 999-9999-9999.
HANSEL: All right, don't tell me.

When's the cheapest time to ring your friends?
When they're out!

Knock, knock.
Who's there?
Ooze.
Ooze who?
Ooze mobile phone was that?

What goes in pink and comes out blue?
A swimmer on a cold day.

Why couldn't the bicycle stand up for itself?
It was two-tyred.

What do you call a sheep that says, 'Moo'?
Bilingual.

What do you call a camel with three humps?
Humphrey.

What do you call a camel at the North Pole?
Lost!

'Doctor, doctor, I think I'm invisible!'
'Who said that?'

'Doctor, doctor, I feel like a pack of cards,'
'I'll deal with you later.'

JO: Why do you call your boyfriend Fog?
MO: Because he's thick and wet.

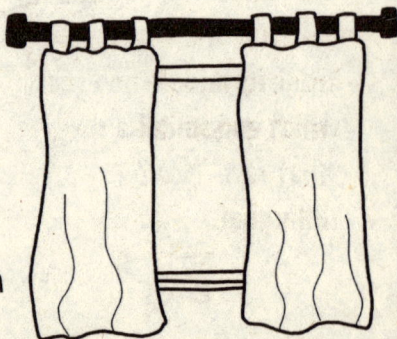

'Doctor, doctor, I feel like a pair of curtains.'
'Pull yourself together.'

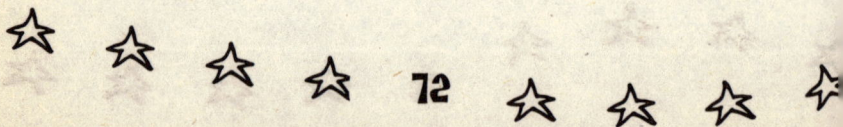

How can you stop moles digging up your garden?
Hide their spades.

Why can't a car play football?
Because it's only got one boot.

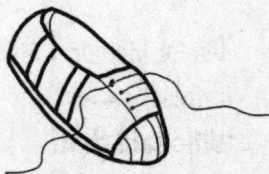

What should you do if you get too hot at a football match?
Sit next to a fan.

How can you tell which end of a worm is the head?
Tickle its middle and see which end smiles.

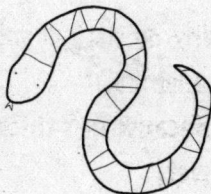

What do you get if you cross a chicken with a bell?
An alarm cluck.

Where do cows go for their holidays?
Moo York.

What's the best way to raise
an elephant?
With a forklift truck.

What's grey, has four legs
and a trunk?
A mouse going on holiday.

Why did the lobster blush?
Because the seaweed.

What did the earwig say
when it fell off the
windowsill?
"Ere we go.'

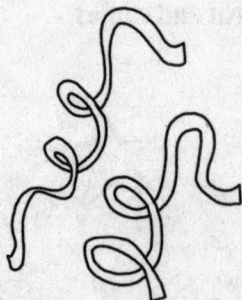

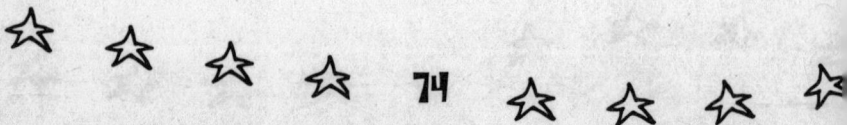

What do you call a fly with no wings?
A walk.

What do you call a man with a paper bag on his head?
Russell.

What do you get if you cross an elephant with a chicken?
A bird that remembers why it crossed the road.

What do bees chew?
Buzzle gum.

How does an octopus go into battle?
Well armed.

What did the boy centipede say to the girl centipede?
'You sure have a nice pair of legs, pair of legs, pair of legs ...'

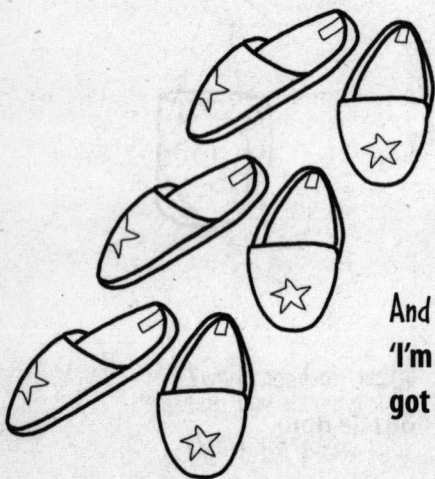

What did the boy millipede say to the girl millipede?
'You sure have a nice pair of legs, pair of legs, pair of legs, pair of legs, pair of legs, pair of legs, pair of legs, pair of legs, pair of legs, pair of legs ...'

And what did she reply?
'I'm not quite ready yet, I've got to put my shoes on.'

Why is tennis such a noisy game?
Because every player raises a racket.

Knock, knock.
Who's there?
Tennis.
Tennis who?
Tennis five plus five.

'Doctor, can you help
me out?'
**'Of course, which way
did you come in?'**

'Doctor, can you give me
something for my liver?'
'How about some onions?'

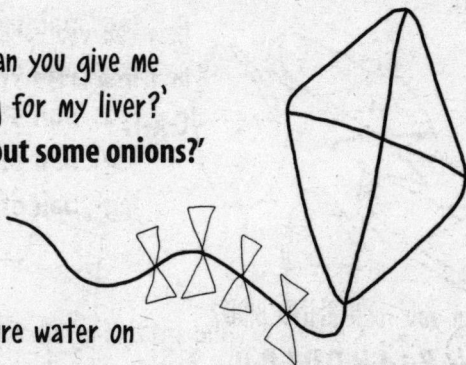

How can you cure water on
the brain?
With a tap on the head.

'Doctor, can you give me
something for wind?'
'Yes, here's a kite.'

BRIAN: If frozen water is iced
water, what is frozen ink?
BRENDA: Iced ink.
BRIAN: I know you do!

Why did the boy wear his trousers inside out?
There were holes on the other side.

What kind of song do you sing
in a car?
A cartoon.

How can you spell MOUSETRAP
in three letters?
C-A-T.

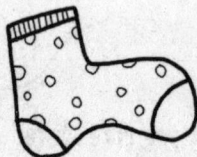

SAL: Can you spell BLIND BIRD?
VAL: Yes. B-L-I-N-D B-I-R-D.
SAL: No, it's B-L-N-D B-R -D.
If it had two 'I's it wouldn't
be blind!

FIRST MOTHER: I'm going to
call my baby Orson, after
Orson Welles.
**SECOND MOTHER: What's
your surname?**
FIRST MOTHER: Kart.

How can you catch a squirrel?
Climb a tree and act like a nut.

Why did the robot eat
paperclips?
They were his staple diet.

DAN: That star up there is
called the Dog Star.
ANNE: You can't be Sirius!

Why did Sally give up her
tap-dancing classes?
**Because she kept falling in
the sink.**

What has six legs and can't
walk?
Three pairs of trousers.

NEDDIE: I used to be twins.
TEDDY: How do you know?
NEDDIE: My mum has a photo of me when I was two.

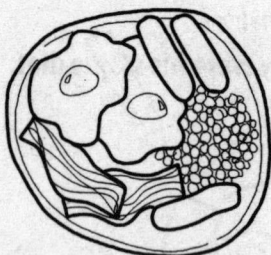

What's an astronaut's
favourite meal?
Launch.

DARREN: My girlfriend's a
twin.
**SHARON: How do you tell
them apart?**
DARREN: Her brother has a
beard.

What's the difference
between a buffalo and a bison?
**You can't wash your hands in
a buffalo.**

What's black and white and
red all over?
A sunburned penguin.

What goes zzub, zzub?
A bee flying backwards.

What happens if someone
swallows the film out of a
camera?
With luck, nothing develops.

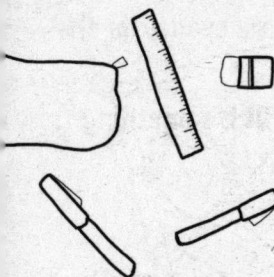

'Doctor, doctor, my baby's just
swallowed my pen. What shall I do?'
'Use a pencil until I get there.'

What did the balloon say to
the pin?
'Hi there, buster!'

What goes 99 plonk, 99 plonk?
**A centipede with a wooden
leg.**

What's white and goes up?
A snowflake with no sense of direction.

Why do cows wear bells?
Their horns don't work.

What did one eye say to the other eye?
'Between us is something that smells.'

Why is a rabbit's nose shiny?
Because its powder puff is at the wrong end.

MUM: Who was that at the door?
DAVE: A man with a drum.
MUM: Tell him to beat it.

What's the difference between a cat and a comma?
A cat has claws at the end of its paws; a comma is a
pause at the end of a clause.

Why does a horse have six legs?
Because it's got forelegs in front
and two legs behind.

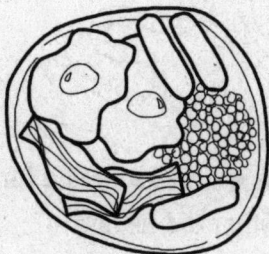

How can you stop a cockerel
crowing on Monday morning?
Eat him for Sunday lunch.

If a buttercup is yellow, what
colour is a hiccup?
Burple.

How do you make a
bandstand?
Take away their chairs.

What do you get if you cross a carpet with an elephant?
A great big pile on your living-room floor.

What is a mermaid?
A deep she-fish.

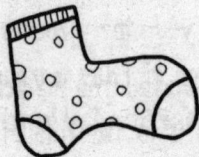

A man walked into a bar.
What did he say?
'Ouch!'

What do you get if you cross
a sheep with a thunderstorm?
A wet blanket.

A family of tortoises went to a cafe for some ice cream. Mother ordered vanilla ice cream, Father ordered raspberry ripple and young Tommy ordered strawberry.

As they were about to eat their ice creams, Mother looked out of the window and said, 'It looks as if it will rain. Will you just nip home, please, Tommy, and fetch an umbrella?'

So Tommy set off. Two days later he still hadn't returned. 'You know,' said Mother Tortoise to Father Tortoise, 'I think we'd better eat Tommy's ice cream before it melts.'

A voice floated towards them from the cafe's entrance. 'If you do that, I won't go!' said Tommy.

A luxury cruise ship took its passengers round the world in style. It had comfortable cabins, wonderful food, and a number of performers who entertained them every evening. Among the performers was a magician whose favourite trick was to make things disappear.

One of the ship's crew had a parrot who hated the magician. Each time he did his act, the parrot would fly to the side of the stage, perch on the scenery, and squawk, 'He's a phoney!'

One night there was a terrible storm, and the ship sank. All that remained was a single plank of wood, on one end of which sat the parrot, and on the other end of which sat the magician. The parrot eyed the magician. 'OK, clever clogs,' he said, 'what did you do with the ship?'

What do you call a
keen gardener?
Pete.

What's a
crocodile's
favourite game?
Snap.

What do you call a gossip?
**Someone who lets the chat
out of the bag.**

A cowboy met an Apache Indian who was
sending smoke signals.
'What's the matter?' asked the cowboy.
'We have no water,' replied the Apache.
'Are you praying for rain?' asked the cowboy.
'No,' replied the Apache. 'I'm sending for a
plumber.'

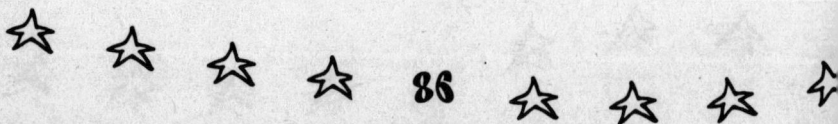

Young Damian was very naughty. All morning he had been running around, getting on his mother's nerves. The last straw came when he climbed a tree and tore his trousers trying to get down again.

'Right,' said his mother. 'Go to your room until lunchtime and play your computer games. While you do so, I'll mend your trousers.'

Half an hour later she heard a noise in the cellar. 'You bad boy,' she called, 'are you running about down there with no trousers on?'

'No, madam,' came a voice, 'I'm reading the gas meter.'

SWEET DREAMS

YAWN ... NOW IT REALLY IS TIME TO GO TO SLEEP ...

What has four legs but only one foot?
A bed.

HONOR: I once dreamt I was eating a huge marshmallow.
DONNA: What happened?
HONOR: When I woke up I found my pillow had disappeared.

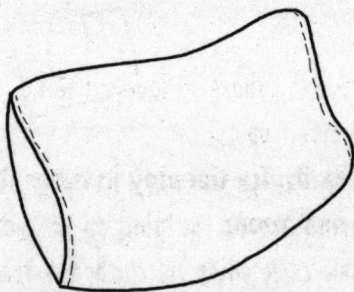

Why did the bed spread?
Because it saw the pillow slip.

Why do people go to bed?
Because the bed won't come to them.

KEITH: I haven't slept for days.
KATE: Why not?
KEITH: I sleep at night.

TIM: Do you still walk in your sleep?
JIM: No, I take my bus fare to bed with me each night.

ALEX: I snore so loudly I wake myself up.
ALAN: Try sleeping in the next room.

How can you cure sleepwalking?
Cover the floor with drawing-pins.

What question can you never answer 'yes' to truthfully?
'Are you asleep?'

HAMISH: Do you always snore?
DOUGAL: Only when I'm asleep.

Knock, knock.
Who's there?
Anna.
Anna who?
Anna nother thing, how many times do I have to tell you to stop snoring?

MUM: Why did you put a mouse in your sister's bed?
WINSTON: Because I couldn't find a frog.

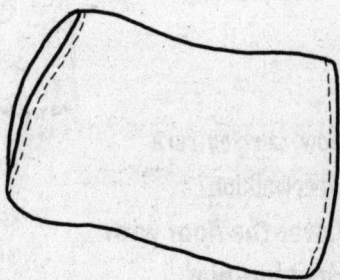

Why did Herbert sleep under a car?
Because he wanted to wake up oily in the morning.

Why did Harold put his bed in the fireplace?
So he could sleep like a log.

MRS MUDDLEHEAD: I'd like to buy a bed.
SHOP ASSISTANT: Spring mattress?
MRS MUDDLEHEAD: No, I want to use it all year round.

A neighbour met young Laura playing outside one evening. 'Isn't it time for little girls to be in bed?' she asked.

'I don't know,' said Laura, 'I haven't got any little girls.'

GILL: Which side do you sleep on, left or right?
HIL: Both, all of me goes to sleep at the same time.

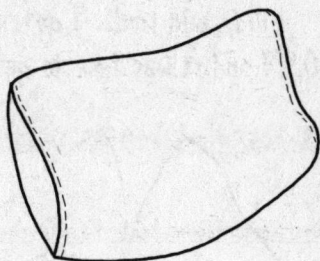

Why did the boy wake up with the room spinning?
He'd slept like a top.

Gareth's mum took him to see the doctor because he had problems with sleeping. 'What's the trouble?' asked the doctor.

'Every night I dream about a door with a sign on it,' said Gareth. 'I pull and pull at the door, but it won't open.'

'What does the sign on the door say?' asked the doctor.

'Push,' answered Gareth.

DANIEL: How much sleep do you usually need?
NATHANIEL: About half an hour more.

When young Linda couldn't sleep her mother told her to count sheep.

'I did,' said Linda. 'I got to 10,987 and it was time to get up.'

Knock, knock.
Who's there?
Scold.
Scold who?
Scold in here now the heating's gone off.

RHONA: Are you asleep?
MONA: I'm not telling you.

Knock, knock.
Who's there?
Norma Lee.
Norma Lee who?
Norma Lee I go to bed at nine
o'clock but tonight Mum let
me stay up.

Annie, Barbie and Carol were all spending the
night with their friend Donna. The problem was,
there was only one spare bed in Donna's house.
So they all squashed into it together.

After a while of tossing and turning, Carol
decided it might be better to sleep on the floor,
where she could stretch out. She was just
getting comfortable when Barbie said to her,
'You might as well get back in bed, Carol,
there's much more room now.'

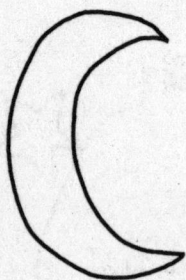

Knock, knock.
Who's there?
Alison.
Alison who?
Alison to my favourite CDs
while I get ready for bed.

Knock, knock.
Who's there?
Eddie.
Eddie who?
Eddie body in bed yet?

Knock, knock.
Who's there?
Yolanda.
Yolanda who?
Yolanda me your pillow, mine's
fallen off the bed.

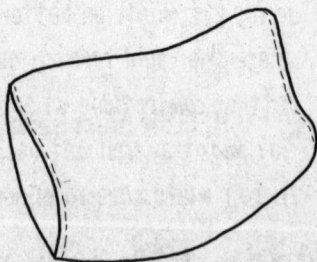

Knock, knock.
Who's there?
Betty.
Betty who?
Betty let me go to sleep, I'm
tired.

FREDDIE: Why do you sleep in your raincoat?
TEDDY: My hot-water bottle leaks.

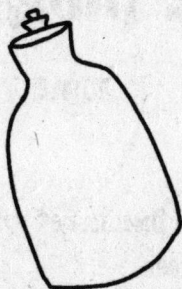

How can you stop yourself falling out of bed?
Sleep on the floor.

NEIL: I heard a loud noise this morning.
NELL: It must have been the crack of dawn.

THE MORNING AFTER

TIME TO GET UP . . .

MUM: Ben! It's time to get up!
It's seven-fifteen.
BEN: Which side's winning?

MUM: Did you wake up grumpy
this morning?
MAGGIE: No, I let him go on
sleeping.

SHARON: How did you sleep
last night?
KAREN: With my eyes
closed.

LYNNE: How fast does light
travel?
GWYN: I don't know, but it
always arrives too early in
the morning.

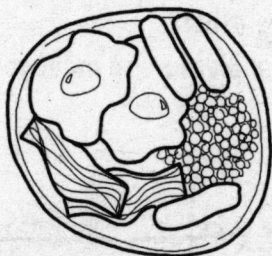

What two things should you never eat before breakfast?
Lunch and dinner.

Why is breakfast in bed so easy to make?
It's just a few rolls and a turnover.

What do cats eat for breakfast?
Mice krispies.

What do French children eat for breakfast?
Huit heures bix.

What do corn flakes wear on their feet?
K'logs.

What did one shredded wheat say to the other?
'Cereal pleasure to meet you.'

Two flies settled on a cereal packet. 'Why are you runnning so fast?' asked one.
'Because,' replied the other, 'it says here, "Tear along the dotted line".'

What is streaky bacon?
A pig running around with no clothes on.

What would happen if pigs could fly?
Bacon would go up.

Knock, knock.
Who's there?
Howell.
Howell who?
Howell you have your bacon, grilled or fried?

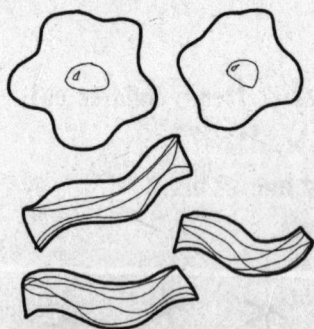

Knock, knock.
Who's there?
Ahab.
Ahab who?
Ahab two sausages with my bacon today.

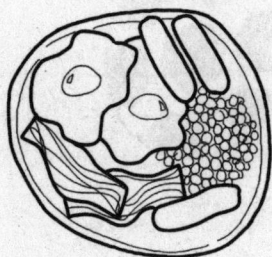

How do you spell ham and eggs
in three letters?
MNX.

**Why are sausages
bad-mannered?**
They spit in the frying-pan.

Knock, knock.
Who's there?
Dozen.
Dozen who?
Dozen anybody know how to
boil an egg?

Knock, knock.
Who's there?
Egbert.
Egbert who?
Egbert who?
Egbert no bacon, please.

FIRST EGG BOILING IN SAUCEPAN: Phew! It's hot in here!
SECOND EGG BOILING IN SAUCEPAN: You wait until you get out, they bash your head in.

Why are scrambled eggs like a poor football team?
They're both beaten.

What's as tall as a tower block and contains thousands of eggs?
A multi-storey omelette.

HARVEY: Did you hear the joke about the three eggs?
HAMISH: No.
HARVEY: Two bad.

What do you call a mischievous egg?
A practical yolker.

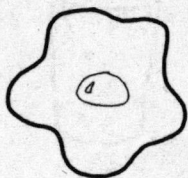

What goes up brown or white and comes down yellow and white?
An egg.

What kind of motorbike can cook eggs?
A scrambler.

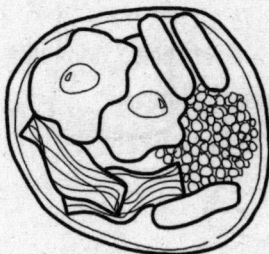

How do monkeys make toast?
Put it under the gorilla.

What did the toaster say to the bread?
'Pop up and see me sometime.'

Why is hot toast like a caterpillar?
It's the grub that makes the butter fly.

Knock, knock.
Who's there?
Juliet.
Juliet who?
Juliet all my toast, may I have some more, please?

What did the baby bird say when he found an orange in his nest?
'Look what marmalade!'

BRENDA: Did you hear the joke about the bread rolls?
GLENDA: No.
BRENDA: Oh, crumbs.

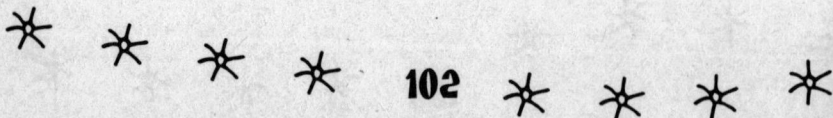

OLLIE: Did you hear the joke about the butter?

POLLY: No.

OLLIE: I'd better not spread it around.

Tommy and Timmy were helping themselves to apples after breakfast. 'Mum,' said Tommy, 'is it true that an apple a day keeps the doctor away?'

Before she could reply, Timmy answered, 'It does if you throw it hard enough.'

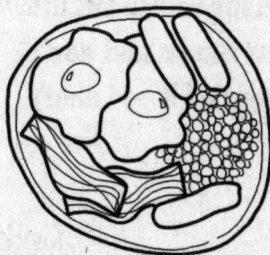

Knock, knock.

Who's there?

Owen.

Owen who?

Owen am I going home again?

103

MUM: Did you thank Mrs Brown for letting you stay?
BELINDA: No.
MUM: Why not?
BELINDA: Well, three of us stayed, and when Annie, who was in front of me, said 'thank you' to Mrs Brown, Mrs Brown said 'don't mention it' so I didn't.

Knock, knock.
Who's there?
Allgood.
Allgood who?
Allgood things must come to an end!

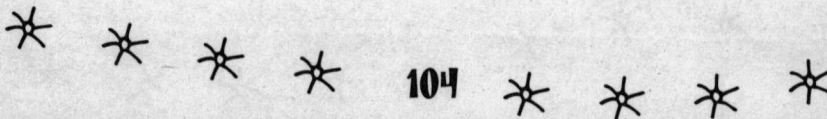